TROLL BOOK

Michael Berenstain

Random House

New York

Library of Congress Cataloging in Publication Data
Berenstain, Michael. The troll book.
SUMMARY: Examines the distinctive features, habits, and neighbors of the troll.
1. Trolls—Juvenile literature. [1. Trolls] I. Title.
GR555.B47   398.2′1   79-5268
ISBN: 0-394-84295-2 (trade); 0-394-94295-7 (lib. bdg.)
Manufactured in the United States of America   1 2 3 4 5 6 7 8 9 0

Deep in the forests of Scandinavia, where the
dark pines loom and pale lichens spot the rocks,
there dwell a strange and little-known folk. No one
knows how long they have been there, nor how
they first came into the world. But it is clear that
they are an ancient race—so ancient, in fact, that
the pines, the lichens, even the rocks feel young
when they pass by.

They are the trolls.

Trolls are usually quite large—over six feet tall—
and, by human standards, not very handsome. Nor
are they very intelligent. Nonetheless, trolls are
perfectly adapted for life in the forest.

Their wide, flat feet
are ideal for tramping
through the deep snows
of the northern winters.

Their long, keen noses are
useful for tracking game.

And, with their big,
furry ears they can hear
a wolf's heartbeat at
fifty paces.

A thick leathery hide is good to have during the hot summer months when mosquitoes begin to swarm.

A long tail comes in handy sometimes.

Trolls are very strong – no one knows just how strong. They probably don't even know themselves.

Like many other large, powerful creatures – bears, rhinoceroses, elephants – trolls have poor eyesight. This is the origin of the old trollish saying, "He couldn't tell a tree from a troll-in-the-ground."

Beyond the forest lies the tundra—a vast frozen
plain stretching, boundless, to the north. Whenever
a troll must cross this icy desert, he usually asks a
reindeer for a lift. Reindeer are easily imposed upon
(if asked politely) and never get lost.

Skiing is an ancient trollish art that has been adapted
by human beings to their own use. Early troll skis
were made of mammoth tusks. Many are still in use,
having been handed down over the
years as family heirlooms. Trolls have never
practiced downhill skiing—it's much too scary.

Trolls build boats of a sort. Oars and sails, however, are considered unnecessary.

In the heart of the forest, the great troll trees stand. At one time, trolls dug their homes among the twisting roots of these giant evergreens. But gradually, over thousands of years, they have extended their dwellings up into the tree trunks themselves.

The living quarters of most troll trees are in the lower trunk. The old underground rooms are used as kitchens and storerooms. A unique feature is the observation platform near the top of the tree. It serves no real purpose, since the eyesight of trolls isn't good enough to observe much of anything. Still, they take great pleasure in pretending to enjoy the view.

Troll family life is centered in the first-floor room—the "sit room," as it is called. Here, the whole family gathers on a cold winter's night to enjoy the warmth of a roaring fire.

At the head of most troll families there is a grandmother, great-grandmother, or even a great-great-grandmother. They are very old. It's hard to say just how old they are since they always lie about their age. Few will admit to being over 500.

Troll matriarchs are not sweet little old ladies. They are tough old biddies with wills of iron and forearms to match.

Aside from family discipline, their chief occupation is magic.

Troll magic is not an art or craft. It is an ability as natural as seeing or breathing. Chief among its uses is the forging of troll gold. Trolls have no real use for gold—they just like to look at it. And, since finding gold is a great deal of trouble, they simply make it from stones, leaves, or dirt.

Many humans have tried to steal troll gold, only to find, on getting it home, that it has changed back to its original form.

Young troll wives have the difficult task of raising a family while dealing with an iron-willed grandmother. They are, despite this, devoted and affectionate mothers.

Troll children, on the other hand, are absolutely unbearable. Their pranks are the terror of the forest.

Father trolls are avid hunters. Though their woodland craft is on the crude side, they make up in enthusiasm what they lack in skill.

Surprisingly, trolls are expert craftsmen. With the simplest of tools and materials, they make a wide range of useful articles.

Mother trolls spend most
of their time home in the
tree. They cook, clean, sew,
and attend to other chores.

In the evenings, a typical
family will gather around
the fire to tell troll tales.
Granny is usually the most
spellbinding storyteller.

Before bed, the whole
family often climbs to the
observation platform
for a breath of air and a
dim view of the stars.

At first glance, the life of a troll in the depths of the forest may seem to be a happy and carefree existence. But it is not without its difficulties. The human race is the trolls' worst worry. People cut down trees, plow up fields, dam rivers, poison streams, and generally make nuisances of themselves. It's small wonder that when humans move into an area, the trolls move out. Today few places remain where trolls can live in peace.

More than anything else, trolls object to human noise. Church bells, especially, annoy them.

This dislike of loud noises goes back to the time when the trolls' ancestors, the frost giants, did battle with the Norse gods and were defeated by the hammer of Thor, the thunder god.

Centuries ago, when the first Scandinavian churches were being built, trolls often tried to "stop that dratted noise" by hurling huge boulders at the steeples.

They missed.

There is a tale of a troll who actually helped to build a church. His motives, however, were evil.

Holy St. Laurentius of Sweden wished to build a grand church, but could find no one to undertake so large a task. One day, a troll came to him and offered to do the work, provided the saint could guess his name before the church was built. If he could not, then payment would be the "Sun and Moon and both Laurentius' eyes."

Determined to have his church, and certain he would be able to guess the creature's name, the saint agreed. The troll set to work with a will.

Every day, as the church rose higher, St. Laurentius tried to guess the troll's name, and every day he failed. He began to worry about the bargain he had made.

Then one day, as the downcast saint wandered in the forest, he saw a strange light through the trees. Drawing near, he saw a family of trolls dancing about a fire and singing:

"Papa Finn will come home soon
He will bring the Sun and Moon—
Daylight, Nightlight, and,
likewise,
Both Laurentius' eyes!"

Hearing this, the saint hurried back to the church, where the troll was high atop the steeple, mounting a golden cross.

"I say, Finn!" he called. "That cross is crooked!"

Startled at hearing his name, the troll lost his grip and fell with a crash to the earth. And that was an end to him.

Not all trolls are content to make bad bargains with saints. Some take more direct action.

Among them, the Night Trolls are the worst. Nowadays, they are not often seen. But, at one time, these dreadful creatures were the terror of remote Scandinavian villages. Descending upon sleeping hamlets in the dead of night, they would carry the poor villagers off to their mountain strongholds.

The captives of the Night
Trolls were not killed or eaten or
even enslaved – they were simply
turned into trolls.

This was done by rubbing them
with magic troll ointment,
stretching their arms, and howling
into their ears.

After a few months of such treatment,
an ordinary human being could not be
distinguished from the average troll.

Night Trolls, as the name implies, are
active only after dark. They are terrified of
sunlight, and with good cause, for if they are
touched even for a moment by the sun's rays,
they are instantly turned to stone.

The effect of sunlight on Night Trolls has given rise to many legends. Throughout Scandinavia it is believed that odd-shaped boulders are trolls who were caught outside their caves by the sunrise. Another folk tradition has it that the Night Trolls were born of stone in ancient times when stone was still soft and alive. In this view, their transformation by sunlight is merely a return to their original form.

Unfortunately, this quaint belief is pure
fantasy—trolls are almost certainly
descended (though much reduced in size
and number) from the frost giants of old.

Night Trolls are not alone in their evil ways. Trolls of any kind can be dangerous—especially when met on their own ground.

The famous story of the Three Billy Goats Gruff is an example. It is from this tale that the notion of trolls living under bridges has come. Such dwellings, however, are the exception, rather than the rule. In most stories, trolls are shown living in trees, caves, huts, houses, or even castles, but never under bridges. On the other hand, the practice of waylaying travelers with intent to consume seems fairly common.

Of course, not all trolls are evil. Some are really quite pleasant and will go out of their way to be helpful. Such trolls are especially friendly toward children.

If they find a child lost in the woods, they will often take him home, give him a nice bowl of gruel, and entertain him through the night with the troll stomp—the traditional trollish dance. Most children survive this hospitality.

There is one variety of troll that lives in close association
with human beings—the Little Trolls of Denmark.

There are some who deny that these creatures are trolls
at all. They consider them members of the dwarf family—a
contention hotly denied by the dwarves. The Little Trolls
range between two and three feet in height. They wear no
clothing, as their long beards and hair supply all the warmth
they need. They make their homes in hollow stumps,
abandoned animal burrows, and sometimes beneath the
floors of barns and farmhouses.

Little Trolls are highly mischievous, delighting in playing jokes on their human neighbors.

In some places, it is traditional for farm households to set out a banquet on Christmas Eve for the benefit of the local trolls. If the farmers neglect this hospitality, the trolls are sure to plague them unmercifully during the following year.

Trolls are not the only mysterious inhabitants of the deep forest. They share their world with a wide range of curious beings—the beings known as the Hidden Folk.

A strange tale is told of the origins of the Hidden
Folk. One day, in the beginning of the world, when Eve
was washing her children in a spring, the Lord appeared
to her. Startled and frightened, she hid those of her
children who were not yet washed. When the Lord asked
her if all her children were there, she answered yes,
hoping to avoid his anger should he find that they were
not all washed. But the Lord knew what she had done
and said that those she had hidden would remain so
forever. At that moment, the unclean children vanished
and were hidden in the hills. From these descended the
Hidden Folk.

Among the Hidden Folk, the elves are most famed. Yet, humankind knows very little about them. They are not of small size; rather, they are close to human height, though far beyond human beauty. Elves do not exist in our space or time. They can enter our world at will, but we cannot reach theirs.

Dwarves are chiefly miners and craftsmen. Since they rarely come aboveground, many legends have sprung up about them. It is often said, for instance, that they have no womenfolk—a notion inspired by the fact that dwarf women look just like dwarf men, complete with beards.

Tomtes are distinctly Scandinavian beings who live in human homes. They guard the household from disaster. But tomtes are not always loyal. If, for instance, a farmer mistreats his livestock, his tomte might cause a bad harvest or sickness.

Skogsra are evil wood spirits who take the form of beautiful women to tempt men to their doom. Their most striking feature is their lack of a back. They have been described as looking like water troughs from the rear.

Another dangerous creature is the nack—a spirit that lives in lakes, rivers, and streams. The nack is unpredictable, at best.

Trolls are on fairly good terms with their neighbors, but they reserve their greatest respect for the elves, who, for their part, regard the trolls with an amused tolerance.

Trolls are now a hidden race, unseen and unknown, their very existence doubted by some. Only in the forgotten corners of the wild do they still survive—places where humankind has never set foot and, perhaps, never will.

In one such spot, a remote valley in the farthest north, Troll Mountain stands. Once the center of a great troll kingdom, it is still the home of the troll king. Here, untouched by the outside world, the trolls preserve their ancient ways.

Troll Mountain was fashioned during the reign
of the first troll king, Bog I. This was the golden
age of the trolls—a time so long ago that it seems
ancient even to the trolls.

The mountain's interior is a maze of halls and
rooms, passages and stairways. Around its base lies
Trollington—a busy town burrowed out from
among the mountain's foothills.

Troll Mountain was long protected from prying eyes by its sheer isolation. But now, the trolls have to deal with the menace of flying machines. At the first sound of an engine in the distance they set to work, making the mountain look like a part of the natural terrain.

Less visible from the air are the
many trollsteads that dot the
countryside. Most are modest
farms with a few head of musk
ox and, perhaps, a moose or two.

Troll mills are also common. They are used
to grind pine cones, the principal troll crop,
into flour.

The gate to the town is well guarded.
A password ("Greetings!") must be given
to gain entrance.

The road to Troll Mountain
leads up to the main toe-stair.

The mountain's entrance is very hard to reach. This is intended to discourage would-be attackers, but it also tends to cut down on casual visitors.

The draw-spoon is the mountain's last line of defense. Above, the crown is patrolled by picked troops.

A Troll Soldier

The mouth-gate opens into the mountain's dim interior.

The lower levels may be reached by express bucket.

A great hall in the center of the mountain serves as an intersection for the many branching tunnels and stairways.

Troll Food

Rat Cake

Old Crow

One passage leads to the kitchens, where food for a feast is being prepared.

Fly Soup

Squash

Tossed Salad

Troll Tools

Sandpaper · Hack saw · File · Drill · Tongs · Vise · Punch · Hammer · Anvil

Farther down, the smiths are at work, forging armor for the king's knights.

Even lower, in the very heart of the mountain, are the dungeons. Here, violators of the Troll Code are held. The Troll Code is a collection of simple rules that govern troll behavior: "Thou shalt not club." "Thou shalt not stomp." "Thou shalt not covet thy neighbor's musk ox."

Lowest of all, deep among the mountain's roots, stretches the Great Grotto. Here, many of the trolls of the Royal Court come to sit in boats upon the dark lake and listen to the peaceful sound of gently dripping water.

From the depths of the grotto,
a narrow stairway climbs to the
mountain's upper levels.

In the Royal Throne Room, a ceremony is in progress. The present king, Bog XXXVIII, is about to knight a loyal soldier of the guard.

A troll knight is expected to perform deeds of gallantry. Troll maidens often benefit from a knight's devotion to duty.

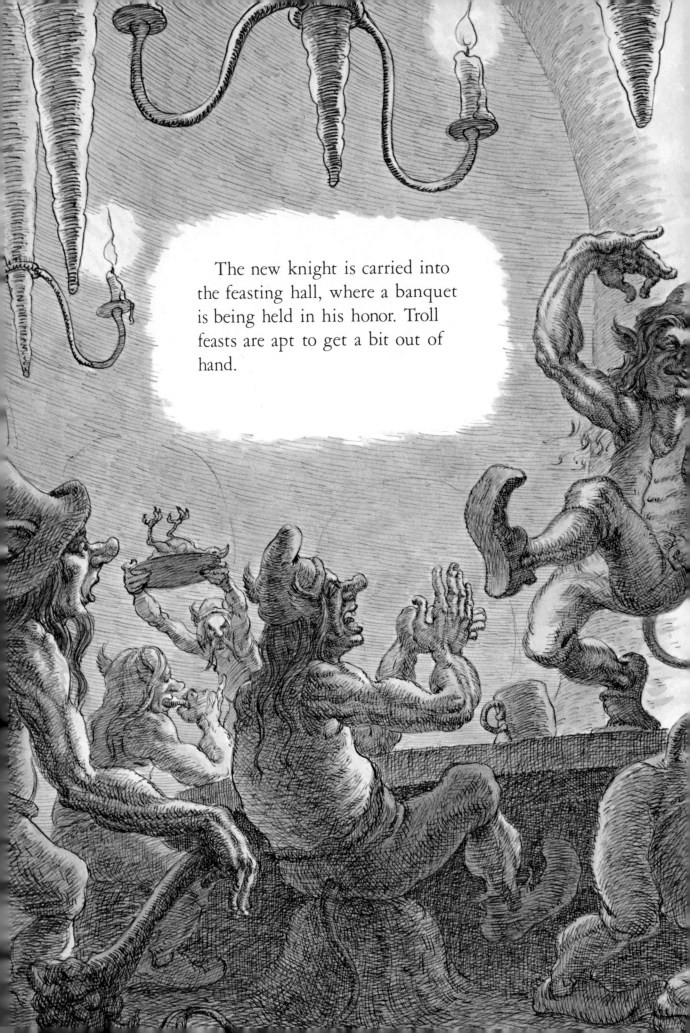

The new knight is carried into the feasting hall, where a banquet is being held in his honor. Troll feasts are apt to get a bit out of hand.

After such a banquet, everyone
is naturally a little tired.

It's left to the
night watchtroll to
put out the candles and
feed the porcupine.

The draw-spoon is raised, the teeth are lowered,
and Troll Mountain retires for the night.